OUR INVENTORS

HISTORIC AFRICAN AMERICAN INVENTORS

KAYVON WEBSTER
Co-Author: Ross Williams

Author

IG: @kayvon

Website: www.williamscommerce1.com/kayvonwebster

Publisher

Williams Commerce, LLC

IG: @wcwriting1

Website: Williamscommerce1 .com

ISBN: 979-8-9895223-6-1

Dedication

This book is dedicated to historical African American inventors and everyone striving to create a better future.

Table of Contents

Intro

Creating is a daily practice of human nature. Every day, we create our futures and legacies by our thoughts and actions. When I was injured during my NFL career, I knew I would have to create a new career path. My helpful words on social media planted the seeds for my literary career. Positive tweets during tough times provided others and myself with the strength and inspiration to fight through adversity.

Early in my entrepreneurship journey, I learned that adversity is a part of every season. The more important lesson was that the rewards of overcoming adversity are worth the sacrifices. I retired from football in 2020 and had my sights on becoming an author and restaurant owner. My career change happened during one of the most significant transitions in world history.

During the pandemic, I came across a God-sent topic. My life was never the same once I began learning about the numerous and magnificent contributions black inventors made to society. Their impacts were too monumental not to be celebrated and covered in schools. As I learned about *Our Inventors*, I became inspired to spotlight their achievements, help others learn about them, and assist readers create the futures they desire.

Leonard Bailey

1825 - 1918

Inventor and entrepreneur **Leonard Bailey** shows how far following your passion can take you. Bailey's breakthrough occurred in 1869 when he served on the first integrated jury. He was 44 years old at the time. Until then, barbering was his primary focus.

During the 1870s, he became known as a successful businessman in the Washington D.C. area. He evolved from a journeyman barber to a seasoned entrepreneur involved in several endeavors. In 1883, Bailey patented a truss-and-bandage that supported patients with hernias. Unlike most inventors, Bailey capitalized on his invention. The US Army Medical Board utilized his creation and provided funding for Bailey's businesses and inventions.

During the 19th century, an array of systemic measures was implemented to stop the economic progress of Black Americans. Banks denied their services to Black families and entrepreneurs. Bailey's greatness extended past innovation. He provided financial assistance for numerous African Americans rejected by lending institutions.

Leonard Bailey played a major role in helping establish the first black-owned bank – The True Reformers Bank. Also, Bailey invented a device adopted by the US Postal Service and another invention utilized by the military. All of Bailey's accomplishments started with his initial passion for barbering.

Lesson #1	Lesson #2	Lesson #3	Lesson #4
Never get content.	Monetize your talents.	Remain persistent and patient.	Don't box yourself in. Just because you are good at one thing doesn't mean you can't be great at other things.

Your Takeaways:

....

....

....

....

....

....

....

Patricia Bath

1942 - 2019

P atricia Era Bath walked into her calling at a young age. Her growth shows the importance of exposure. Bath's parents invested in their daughter's education and passionate commitment to a life in medicine. **Patricia Bath** experienced success early in the science realm. In high school, her cancer research earned her placement on the front page of the New York Times.

After obtaining her medical degree with honors from Howard University in 1968, she interned at Harlem Hospital. The next major move of her career showed how great things happen when we use our influence for positive reasons. Bath influenced Harlem Hospital Eye Clinic to offer eye surgery services and persuaded her professors at Columbia University to operate on blind patients for free.

One of her most impactful findings occurred when she conducted a study that concluded blindness rates among Black Americans doubled the rates of White Americans. She attributed the results to a lack of access to ophthalmic care.

Bath pioneered a discipline known as community ophthalmology, which combines public health, community medicine, and clinical ophthalmology to offer primary care to under-serviced populations. Patricia Bath's extraordinary creativity skills and extensive research led to the invention of a new device and technique for cataract surgery known as laserphaco and the ability to recover the sight of people who were blind for 30+ years.

Lesson #1	Lesson #2	Lesson #3	Lesson #4
Leverage support.	Be unapologetic about your greatness.	Overcoming obstacles leads to new heights.	The impossible is possible.

Your Takeaways:

....

....

....

....

....

....

....

Marie Van Brittan Brown

1922 - 1999

One of the most impactful methods to succeed in business is to identify a problem and present a solution. **Marie Van Brittan Brown** was a lifelong resident of Jamacia Queens, New York, and the inventor of the first home security system and closed-circuit television. In the 1960s, she identified a common problem in inner-city neighborhoods - law enforcement response times and created a solution.

Marie Brown worked as a nurse, and her husband, Albert Brown, was an electronics technician. Their schedules kept them away from their houses for extended periods. Marie and Albert worked together to establish a safer society and home by creating the first security system.

Marie Brown's invention initially consisted of four peepholes for different heights, a camera, monitors, a two-way microphone, and an alarm button to alert the police immediately. These items created a closed-circuit television system for surveillance, also known as CCTV. The patent for her security system was filed in 1966 and heavily influenced the modern-day home security system.

The New York Times covered Brown in a viral article published on December 6, 1969. The 70s appeared to be a launching pad for Marie Brown's career. However, media coverage died down after her successful patent application and major interview.

Even more unfortunate, Brown was not able to profit from the commercialization of her creation. The home security industry is roughly valued at $1.5 billion and will continue to grow. Her invention plays a major role in protecting people worldwide and is utilized in most households and businesses across the country.

Lesson #1

Teamwork makes the dream work.

Lesson #2

The best inventions come from presenting a solution to a problem.

Lesson #3

If you do not profit off your invention, others will.

Lesson #4

Capitalize on momentum and oppertunities because they won't always be there.

Your Takeaways:

....

....

....

....

....

....

....

Alfred Cralle

1866 - 1919

Ice cream entered dining rooms across the country during the 19th century. While presidents such as George Washington, Thomas Jefferson, and James Madison were documented eating ice cream, it was a delicacy at the time. **Alfred Cralle** changed that and helped ice cream reach its commercialized success.

Cralle was born in Virginia on September 4, 1866. Throughout his upbringing, he worked with his father doing carpentry work and attended local schools. His exposure to carpentry made him interested in mechanics.

After attending Wayland Seminary, an institute created to educate newly freed slaves after the Civil War, Cralle moved to Pittsburg, Pennsylvania. His first job in the new city led him to become a historic inventor. While employed at a hotel, he observed that servers had trouble with ice cream sticking to serving spoons.

To provide a solution and make his co-workers' jobs easier, Cralle developed an ice cream scoop. Before his invention, servers needed two hands and instruments to extract and serve ice cream.

Cralle did not financially capitalize on his invention, but his historic achievements were not in vain. Cralle's success as an inventor and entrepreneur helped dispel demeaning characterizations utilized to stereotype African Americans following the end of the Civil War.

Lesson #1	Lesson #2	Lesson #3	Lesson #4
Prepare for success.	Pay close attention to your surroundings.	Think outside of the box.	Catch trends early.

Your Takeaways:

....

....

....

....

....

....

....

Dr. George Grant

1846 – 1910

Dr. George Grant became the second African American to earn a degree from Harvard Dentistry School in 1868. Three years later, Grant was hired by the Department of Mechanical Dentistry and became Harvard University's first African American faculty member. He became an inventor when he created inserts for patients with cleft palates. Dr. Grant's work gained international fame in the dental community, and he began his own practice.

Dr. George Grant's innovative genius extended beyond his medical accomplishments. He developed a love for golf and made the game easier and more enjoyable by creating the wooden tee. Dr. Grant manufactured his inventions locally and distributed them to friends and playing partners.

Although his creation is one of the most essential pieces of sporting equipment, Grant didn't receive recognition until decades after his death. Ironically, another dentist commercialized and capitalized on Grant's invention. In 1991, the United States Golf Association recognized Dr. Grant as the original inventor of the wooden tee.

Lesson #1	Lesson #2	Lesson #3	Lesson #4
Don't underestimate your creations.	Consult with professionals in other industries.	Build a team.	Broadcast your wins.

Your Takeaways:

....

....

....

....

....

....

....

Robert Francis Flemming Jr.

1839 – 1919

Robert Francis Flemming Jr. was an inventor and a sailor in the Civil War. Flemming's initial popularity stemmed from his days as a sailor. While aboard the USS Housatonic ship, he was the first crew member to spot a submarine that caused the first sinking of an enemy ship during the Civil War.

After his tenure in the military, he returned to Massachusetts and worked as a guitar manufacturer and a guitar teacher. On March 30, 1886, Flemming invented a guitar called the euphonica. He believed it produced a louder and more profound sound than the traditional guitar.

One year later, on April 5, 1887, he received a Canadian patent. His success influenced him to start a business and play music in front of it. Customers and civilians were enamored by the music he played.

At the turn of the 20th century, **Robert Flemming** retired, but continued providing lessons and performing at various functions. In 1907, he composed a legendary masterpiece titled the "National Funeral Hymn." Robert Flemming died in February 1919 and is credited with inventing the modern-day acoustic guitar.

Lesson #1	Lesson #2	Lesson #3	Lesson #4
Aim for international success.	Embrace opportunities to do brave acts.	Don't get content.	Expand on traditions.

Your Takeaways:

....

....

....

....

....

....

....

Willis Johnson

1857 - 1923

Willis Johnson's legacy embodies the importance of documenting our experiences. He created an invention that lived on for centuries. However, not much is known about his life.

Johnson was born into slavery during 1857 in Cincinnati, Ohio. Despite oppression, he was still able to become successful. Prior to his invention, eggs, and other mixable ingredients were mixed by hand. That process was labor-intensive and time-consuming.

Willis Johnson's invention was more than just an eggbeater. His device was created to mix eggs, batter, and other baker's ingredients and had a double-acting machine with two chambers. Johnson's invention saved time and energy and served as a model for electrical beaters and mixers.

Lesson #1	Lesson #2	Lesson #3	Lesson #4
Document your journey.	Someone always has it worse.	Don't let adversity stop you.	Work smarter, not harder.

Your Takeaways:

....

....

....

....

....

....

....

Lonnie Johnson

(1949)

D id you know that an African American man created one of the most popular and best-selling toys ever? **Lonnie Johnson** is a prolific rocket scientist and inventor. As a child, the Super Soaker inventor was nicknamed The Professor due to his extraordinary knowledge of mechanical technology and experimentation skills. He built engines out of scrap parts and spent countless hours learning the basics of robotics.

Johnson broke racial barriers when he represented his segregated high school in 1968 as the only black student to compete at a science fair in Alabama. Against all odds, he won first place by creating a compressed-air-power robot known as Linux.

After earning a master's degree in nuclear engineering at Tuskegee University in 1975, Johnson began working for Oak Ridge National Laboratory and the U.S. Air Force, where he pioneered the development of the stealth bomber program.

During the 1980s, he experienced tremendous success while working at NASA. The next decade was a turning point in his career. In 1990, the Super Soaker hit the shelves and quickly became the country's best-selling toy. Currently, Lonnie Johnson owns a technology company with multiple spin-offs and has more than 250 patents.

Lesson #1	Lesson #2	Lesson #3	Lesson #4
Leverage support.	Strive to become the first.	Dream big.	Embrace your differences.

Your Takeaways:

....

....

....

....

....

....

....

....

Frederic McKinley Jones

1893 - 1961

Frederick McKinley Jones overcame numerous obstacles as a youth. He was orphaned at seven and began working at 11. Being independent was more than a way of life for him. This independent assertiveness translated to his education too. Jones became a self-taught auto mechanic at 14 and received his engineering license at 20.

He also had success in the military. While participating in World War I, he earned a promotion to sergeant, worked as an electrician, and taught other soldiers. Sergeant Jones used his wiring skills to provide his camp with electricity, telegraph, and telephone services.

Frederick Jones began innovating shortly after his tenure in the military when he built a transmitter for his town's first radio station. His self-teaching in electronics led to a life-changing invention - a device to combine sound with motion pictures. This idea generated successful partnerships and business deals. Joseph Numero and Frederick Jones worked in tandem. They accomplished numerous achievements together, including the lucrative sale of Jones's movie sound equipment business and the Thermo King Corporation, which was valued at $3 Million in 1949.

During that same year, he received a patent for a portable air-cooling unit. His creation played an intricate part in World War II by preserving blood, medicine, and food at army hospitals and on battlefields. **Fredrick McKinley Jones** was awarded 61 patents, and several of his other notable inventions included a portable X-ray machine, a movie ticket dispenser, a radio service for doctors, a snow machine that attached skis to a propeller-powered snowmobile, and a soundtrack synchronizer.

Lesson #1	Lesson #2	Lesson #3	Lesson #4
Don't feel sorry for yourself.	Charge full price for your talents.	We go further together than apart.	Don't limit yourself.

Your Takeaways:

....

....

....

....

....

....

....

....

Mary Beatrice Davidson Kenner

1912 - 2006

Mary Beatrice Davidson Kenner was born into a family of innovators on May 17, 1912. Her father, maternal grandfather, and sister also earned patents. Kenner holds the record (five) for the most patents by an African American woman.

Racial discrimination was a roadblock for Kenner, but she did not let that stop her. In 1956, she received a patent for the sanitary belt. Several major companies were interested in commercializing her invention, but declined to move forward after discovering she was a black woman. Even more disheartening, she wasn't able to capitalize on her creation because her patent expired. The expiration permitted others the rights to manufacture and sell her product.

Twenty years after her patent for the sanitary belt, Kenner patented an attachment for a walker and wheelchair that included a hard-surfaced tray and a soft pocket for carrying items. During her next invention, she showed the ability to work with a family member. She and her sister, Mildred Davidson, invented a toilet paper holder they patented in 1982.

Her final patent - a mounted back washer and massager was granted on September 29, 1987. Unjustly, **Mary Beatrice Davidson Kenner** didn't receive any awards or formal recognition for her innovative work. However, her historic inventions and contributions distinguished her as a patent record holder and paved the way for subsequent innovations.

Lesson #1	Lesson #2	Lesson #3	Lesson #4
Identify what talents run in your family.	Explore your options.	Time waits on no one.	Learn from your predecessors.

Your Takeaways:

....

....

....

....

....

....

....

Lewis Latimer

1848 - 1928

Lewis Latimer was born in 1842. His father was the first person in his family to receive notoriety when he escaped from slavery and was represented at trial by Frederick Douglass. Eventually, he purchased his freedom.

During early childhood, Lewis Latimer remained under his father's wing while he worked at a barbershop during the day and hung wallpaper at night. After a stint in the U.S. Navy, he secured a job at a patent law firm. By observing draftsmen at work and reading books, Latimer taught himself mechanical drawing.

Latimer's first invention surfaced when he co-patented an improved toilet system for railroad cars called the Water Closet for Railroad Cars. His innovation caught the attention of Thomas Edison and Alexander Graham Bell. Latimer worked closely with Edison and Bell and designed his own inventions.

In 1876, Bell appointed **Lewis Latimer** to draft the required drawings to receive a patent for his invention, the telephone. Latimer's linguistic skills were just as impressive as his innovation skills. He functioned as a German and French translator.

One of Latimer's most popular inventions, the electric lamp, was awarded a patent on September 13, 1881. Four months later, he earned another patent for the "Process of Manufacturing Carbons," an improved method for producing carbon filaments for lightbulbs. In addition to his groundbreaking inventions, Latimer wrote two popular books, played the violin and flute, was a passionate civil rights activist, and was a National Inventors Hall of Fame inductee.

Lesson #1	Lesson #2	Lesson #3	Lesson #4
Seek exposure.	Connect and build with the right people.	Provide value to others.	Make time for productive extra-curricular activities.

Your Takeaways:

....

....

....

....

....

....

....

Jerry Lawson

1940 – 2011

Jerry Lawson revolutionized video games and was one of the few African American electronic engineers who worked in computing at the beginning of the video game era. Lawson led the development of "Fairchild Channel F," the first cartridge-based home video game console system. Before his groundbreaking innovation, video games did not have a pause feature.

At the time, most game systems had game programming built into the hardware, so it could not be removed or changed. **Jerry Lawson** and his team refined and improved technology that allowed games to be stored as software on removable cartridges.

Lawson's dedication to his pursuit was inspirational. In addition to overcoming numerous racial barriers, he remained in the Federal Communication Commission's lobby for three days until someone finally approved his product. Lawson's creation allowed people to play various games in their homes and paved the way for systems such as the Atari 2600, Nintendo, Xbox, and PlayStation.

Lesson #1	Lesson #2	Lesson #3	Lesson #4
Go the extra mile to get the job done.	Pioneer new movements.	Leverage partnerships.	Take chances or miss opportunities.

Your Takeaways:

....

....

....

....

....

....

John Lee Love

1889 - 1931

Could you imagine having to sharpen your pencil with a knife? Thanks to **John Lee Love**, the practice of sharpening your pencil with a knife ended in the 1890s. In 1894, Love invented the hand-cranked pencil sharpener, a portable alternative to contemporary pencil sharpeners. On November 23, 1897, he filed a patent application for the "Love Sharpener."

Prior to inventing the Love Sharpener, Love designed an enhanced plasterer's hawk. His tool increased the safety and productivity of work performed by masons, plasterers, and other handymen. Love's plasterer's hawk was designed with a detachable handle and portable unlike the previous version of one-piece plasterer's hawks.

Although Love hasn't received his deserving share of notoriety, his inventions are still widely used, imitated, and well-known. Love's inventions made this world a more efficient place.

Lesson #1	Lesson #2	Lesson #3	Lesson #4
Improve current methods.	Safety first.	Work smarter, not harder.	Create something to help others.

Your Takeaways:

....

....

....

....

....

....

....

Alexander Miles

1838 - 1918

Alexander Miles has one of the most inspirational reasons for becoming an inventor. His daughter was involved in a life-threatening incident when she fell down an elevator shaft. This prompted him to draft his design for electric-powered elevator doors. The generational wealth-generating patent was awarded on October 11, 1887.

Previously, elevator doors had to be opened and closed manually. The archaic process involved numerous hazards that his daughter almost fell victim to. His elevator patent still influences modern designs and has become a standard feature.

Alexander Miles was a pioneer of the elevator industry and transcended racial barriers in the United States. Miles' innovation made electric-powered elevator doors widely accepted around the world. Before becoming an inventor, Miles was a prominent businessman. At the time of his death on May 7, 1918, he was one of the wealthiest African Americans in the Pacific Northwest region. In 2007, he was inducted into the National Inventors Hall-of-Fame.

Lesson #1	Lesson #2	Lesson #3	Lesson #4
Seek to solve a problem in society.	Seek for opportunities in adversity.	Act on ideas immediately.	Analyze and improve existing methods.

Your Takeaways:

....

....

....

....

....

....

....

Made in the USA
Columbia, SC
25 November 2024

47000380R00035